For Ma and Pa—Love, Mels

2004 First U.S. edition
This selection and arrangement © 2002 by John Foster
Database right Oxford University Press (maker)
Illustrations copyright © 2002 by Oxford University Press
Originally published by Oxford University Press UK in 2002

Published by Charlesbridge
85 Main Street
Watertown, MA 02472
(617) 926-0329
www.charlesbridge.com

Oxford University Press
Great Clarendon Street
Oxford OX2 6DP

Library of Congress Cataloging-in-Publication Data
Drift upon a dream : poems for sleepy babies / compiled by John Foster ;
illustrated by Melanie Williamson.—1st U.S. ed.
p. cm.
Summary: American and English poems for young children about the end of
the day, bedtime, and sleep.
ISBN 1-57091-577-6 (reinforced for library use)
ISBN 1-57091-578-4 (softcover)
1. Night—Juvenile poetry. 2. Sleep—Juvenile poetry. 3. Children's
poetry, American. 4. Children's poetry, English. 5. Lullabies,
American. 6. Lullabies, English. [1. Bedtime—Poetry. 2. Sleep—Poetry.
3. American poetry. 4. English poetry. 5. Lullabies, American. 6.
Lullabies, English. 7. Poetry—Collections.] I. Foster, John, 1941 Oct.
12- II. Williamson, Melanie, ill. III. Title.
PS595.N54D75 2004
811.008'033—dc22   2003017670

Printed in Singapore
(hc) 10 9 8 7 6 5 4 3 2 1
(sc) 10 9 8 7 6 5 4 3 2 1

Illustrations done in acrylic on watercolor paper
Display type and text type set in Bembo and Twinkle
Color separated, printed, and bound by Imago

Acknowledgments: **Gwenda Black:** "Tree Bear," reprinted by permission of Ewan and Ceri Black. Copyright © by Gwenda Black. **Alan Bold:** "Lullaby," from John Foster (ed), *A Very First Poetry Book* (Oxford: OUP, 1984); reprinted by permission of Alice Bold. Copyright © 1984 by Alan Bold. **Charles Causley:** "Climb the Stairs," from Charles Causley, *All Day Saturday* (London: Macmillan, 1994); reprinted by permission of David Higham Associates. **Gina Douthwaite:** "Baby in a Basket," first published as "Lullaby" in John Foster (ed), *My First Book of Oxford Poems* (Oxford: OUP, 2000); reprinted by permission of the author. **Olive Dove:** "How Far," from *Poetry Corner* (London: BBC, 1981); reprinted by permission of Mrs. R. Dean. **Eleanor Farjeon:** "Good Night," from Eleanor Farjeon, *Silver Sand and Snow* (London: Michael Joseph, 1951); reprinted by permission of David Higham Associates. **John Foster:** "Nighttime," from John Foster, *Bare Bear and Other Rhymes* (Oxford: OUP, 1999); by permission of the author. Copyright © 1999 by John Foster. "Lullaby," from John Foster (compiler) *Drift Upon a Dream: Poems for Sleepy Babies* (Oxford: OUP, 2002); by permission of the author. Copyright © 2002 by John Foster. **Lee Bennett Hopkins:** "Night Bear," from Lee Bennett Hopkins (selected by), *Surprises* (New York: HarperCollins, 1972); reprinted by permission of Curtis Brown, Ltd., New York. Copyright © 1972 by Lee Bennett Hopkins. **Eve Merriam:** "You Be Saucer," from Eve Merriam, *You Be Good & I'll Be Night* (New York: Morrow Jr. Books, 1988); reprinted by permission of Marian Reiner on behalf of the author. Copyright © 1988 by Eve Merriam. **Sarojini Naidu:** "Cradle Song," from K. C. Lahiri (ed), *Indo-English Poetry in Bengal* (Oxford: OUP, 1945). Copyright holder not traced. **Barrie Wade:** "Lullaby," from Barrie Wade, *Rainbow* (Oxford: OUP, 1995); reprinted by permission of the author. **Clyde Watson:** "Hush-a-Bye, My Darling," from Clyde Watson, *Catch Me and Kiss Me and Say It Again* (New York: Wm Collins Sons & Co., 1978); reprinted by permission of Curtis Brown, Ltd., New York. Copyright © 1978 Clyde Watson. Although we have tried to trace and contact all copyright holders, this has not been possible in one case. If notified the publishers will be pleased to rectify any errors or omissions at the earliest opportunity.

Drift Upon a Dream

a Dream

Poems for sleepy babies

Chosen by John Foster

Illustrated by

Melanie Williamson

 **Charlesbridge**

The Evening Is Coming

The evening is coming.
The sun sinks to rest.
The birds are all flying
straight home to their nests.
"Caw, caw," says the crow
as he flies overhead.
It's time little children
were going to bed.

Here comes the pony.
His work is all done.
Down through the meadow
he takes a good run.
Up go his heels,
and down goes his head.
It's time little children
were going to bed.

Anonymous

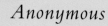

Nighttime

The sun has slipped behind the hill.
The flowers' petals are closed and still.
The birds in the trees are silent now
As they softly settle upon the bough.
In his basket the dog breathes deep,
Puts his head on his paws, and falls asleep.

John Foster

Climb the Stairs

Climb the stairs, Katie,
Climb the stairs, Paul,
The sun is down
On the orchard wall.

All through the valley
The air turns blue,
And silvers the meadow grass
With dew.

High in the tower
The scritch owl cries,
Watching where darkest
Darkness lies.

The bats round the barnyard
Skim and stray
From last of light
To first of day.

Unseen, the water
Winds on the weir
Sings a night song
For all to hear.

Good night, Katie,
Good night, Paul,
Sleep till the new day
Comes to call.

Charles Causley

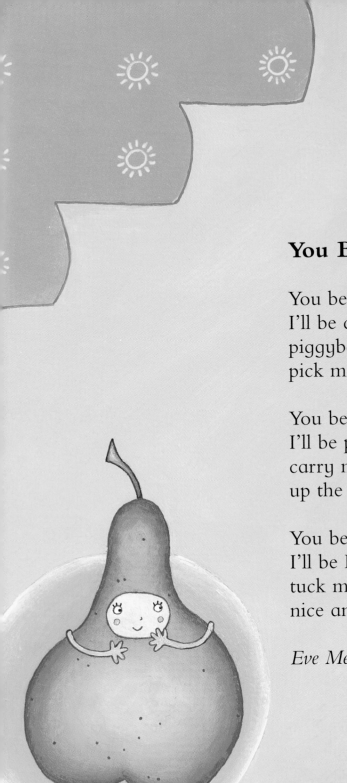

You Be Saucer

You be saucer,
I'll be cup,
piggyback, piggyback,
pick me up.

You be tree,
I'll be pears,
carry me, carry me
up the stairs.

You be Good,
I'll be Night,
tuck me in, tuck me in
nice and tight.

Eve Merriam

Teddy Bear, Teddy Bear

Teddy Bear, Teddy Bear, turn around.
Teddy Bear, Teddy Bear, touch the ground.
Teddy Bear, Teddy Bear, show your shoe.
Teddy Bear, Teddy Bear, that will do.

Teddy Bear, Teddy Bear, go upstairs.
Teddy Bear, Teddy Bear, say your prayers.
Teddy Bear, Teddy Bear, turn out the light.
Teddy Bear, Teddy Bear, say good night.

Traditional

Tree Bear

Listen to the tree bear
Crying in the night,
Crying for his mommy
In the pale moonlight.

What will his mommy do
When she hears him cry?
She'll tuck him in a cocoa pod
And sing a lullaby.

Gwenda Black

Night Bear

In the dark of night
   when all is still
and I'm half sleeping in my bed:

It's good to know
   my teddy bear
is snuggling at my head.

Lee Bennett Hopkins

Star Light

Star light, star bright,
First star I see tonight,
I wish I may, I wish I might,
Have the wish I wish tonight.

Anonymous

Lullaby

The stars have switched their lights on.
Day's curtains have been drawn.
The birds are resting in the trees.
There's dew upon the lawn.

The toys are in their boxes.
The stories have been read.
It's time for drifting off to sleep
Tucked safely up in bed.

John Foster

Rock-a-Bye, Baby

Rock-a-bye, baby,
Thy cradle is green.
Father's a nobleman,
Mother's a queen;
And Betty's a lady
And wears a gold ring;
And Johnny's a drummer
And drums for the king.

Traditional

Hush, Little Baby, Don't Say a Word

Hush, little baby, don't say a word,
Papa's gonna buy you a mockingbird.

And if that mockingbird won't sing,
Papa's gonna buy you a diamond ring.

If that diamond ring turns to brass,
Papa's gonna buy you a looking glass.

If that looking glass gets broke,
Papa's gonna buy you a billy goat.

And if that billy goat falls down,
You'll still be the sweetest little baby in town.

Traditional

How Far

"How far away
Is the evening star?"
"Ask the night horse,
He knows how far.

Talk to him gently.
Give him honey and hay,
Seven bells for his bridle
And he'll take you away.

Snorting white fire
He will stream through the air
Past mountains of the moon
And the rainbow's stairs.

And if you go singing
Through the dark and the cold
Your purse will be filled
With silver and gold."

Olive Dove

Cradle Song

From groves of spice
O'er fields of rice
Athwart the lotus stream
   I bring for you
   Aglint with dew
A little lovely dream.

Sweet, shut your eyes
The wild fireflies
Dance through the fairy neem:
   From the poppy bole
   For you I stole
A little lovely dream.

Dear eyes, good night,
In golden light
The stars around you gleam;
   On you I press
   With soft caress
A little lovely dream.

Sarojini Naidu

Good Night

Now good night.
Fold up your clothes
As you were taught,
Fold your two hands,
Fold up your thought;
Day is the ploughland,
Night is the stream,
Day is for doing
And night is for dream.
Now good night.

Eleanor Farjeon

Baby in a Basket

Baby in a basket
floats upon a stream,
rocks along the river
of a gentle dream,

sails away in slumber
on a cot of rushes
where the lapping of water
soothes and hushes.

Baby in a basket
floats upon a stream,
rocks along the river
of a gentle dream.

Gina Douthwaite

Sandmen, Sandmen

Sandmen, sandmen,
Wise and creepy,
Croon dream songs
To make us sleepy.

A lovely maid with deep dark eyes
Is queen of all their lullabies.
On her ancient moon guitar
She strums a sleep song to a star;
And when the deep dark shadows fall
Snow-white lilies hear her call.

Sandmen, sandmen,
Wise and creepy,
Croon dream songs
To make us sleepy.

Anonymous

Hush-a-Bye, My Darling

Hush-a-bye, my darling
Don't you make a peep,
Little creatures everywhere
Are settling down to sleep.

Fishes in the millpond
Goslings in the barn
Kitten by the fireside
Baby in my arms.

Listen to the raindrops
Singing you to sleep,
Hush-a-bye, my darling
Don't you make a peep.

Clyde Watson

African Lullaby

Sleep, my little one! The night is all wind and rain;
The meal has been wet by the raindrops
   and bent is the sugarcane;
O Giver who gives to the people,
   in safety my little son keep!
My little son with the headdress,
   sleep, sleep, sleep!

Traditional

Lullaby

Close your eyes gently
    And cuddle in
Keep yourself snug, a
    New day will begin.

Have pleasant dreams about
    Those things you love,
Sleep is an island
    Waiting above.

Night is a blanket
    Keeping you warm
If you close eyes you can
    Come to no harm.

Dreams are like journeys
    Drifting along,
Rest is a present
    Keeping you strong.

Alan Bold

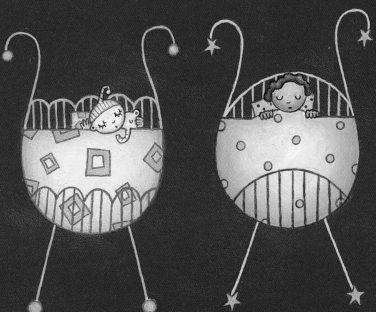

Lullaby

Hush, can you hear
in the thickening deep
the air in the trees
is falling asleep?

Hush, can you see
where the darkening skies
stretch over the sunset
and close heavy eyes?

Hush, can you hear
where the whispering corn
is settling down
and starting to yawn?

Hush, can you see
in the moon's silver beam
the light of the world
beginning to dream?

Hush, can you feel
the whole world give a sigh
and fall fast asleep
to your lullaby?

Barrie Wade

Sweet and Low

Sweet and low, sweet and low,
Wind of the western sea,
Low, low, breathe and blow,
Wind of the western sea!
Over the rolling waters go,
Come from the dying moon, and blow,
Blow him again to me;
While my little one, while my pretty one sleeps.

Sleep and rest, sleep and rest,
Father will come to thee soon;
Rest, rest, on mother's breast,
Father will come to thee soon;
Father will come to his babe in the nest,
Silver sails all out of the west
Under the silver moon;
Sleep, my little one, sleep, my pretty one, sleep.

Alfred, Lord Tennyson